AMAZING MAZES
FOR
MINECRAFTERS

Challenging Mazes for Hours of Entertainment!

JEN FUNK WEBER

Sky Pony Press
New York

Copyright © 2019 by Hollan Publishing, Inc.

Minecraft® is a registered trademark of Notch Development AB.

The Minecraft game is copyright © Mojang AB.

Sky Pony Press books may be purchased in bulk at special discounts for sales promotion, corporate gifts, fund-raising, or educational purposes. Special editions can also be created to specifications. For details, contact the Special Sales Department, Sky Pony Press, 307 West 36th Street, 11th Floor, New York, NY 10018 or info@skyhorsepublishing.com.

Sky Pony® is a registered trademark of Skyhorse Publishing, Inc.®, a Delaware corporation.

Visit our website at www.skyponypress.com.

10 9 8 7 6

Library of Congress Cataloging-in-Publication Data is available on file.

Puzzles and activities by Jen Funk Weber

Cover and interior artwork by Amanda Brack

Book design by Kevin Baier

Print ISBN: 978-1-5107-4723-4

Printed in China

TABLE OF CONTENTS

CAVE EXPLORERS

Four Minecraft players are trying to find their way to a cave where a treasure is hidden. Follow each player's path, under and over crossing paths, to discover which players make it and which one gets lost.

Carlos   **Cara**   **Cami**   **Camilo**

REDSTONE ROUND-UP

Alex has plans to build an epic redstone machine. Help her collect all the redstone in the maze. To do this, draw a line from Start to Finish that passes once through every redstone block and dust mound. Your line can go up, down, left, or right, but not diagonally. On your mark, get set, collect!

Start

Finish

A DOG'S LIFE

Find your way through this maze from START to FINISH. It will be easier if you correctly identify each statement as true or false.

Start

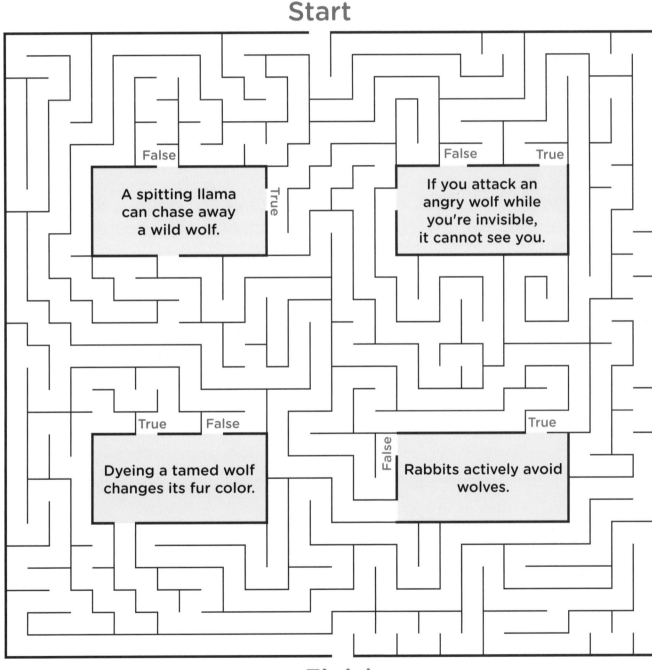

False

A spitting llama can chase away a wild wolf.

True

False True

If you attack an angry wolf while you're invisible, it cannot see you.

True False

Dyeing a tamed wolf changes its fur color.

False

True

Rabbits actively avoid wolves.

Finish

HOP TO IT #1

Find your way from the top-left yellow box to the bottom-right yellow box by keeping one icon the same each time you hop boxes. There are two paths to take. See if you pick the right one!

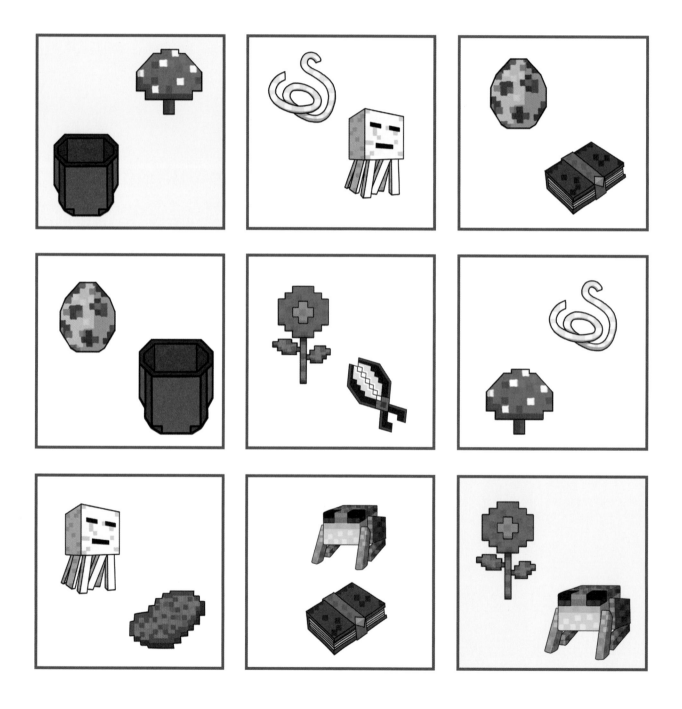

CAPTURE THE SWORD

Navigate this maze to capture the diamond sword in the center. Begin at one corner (you'll have to guess which one), and follow the numbers and arrows.

Each square tells you how many spaces to move and in what direction. Arrows leading off the grid are dead ends. Can you find the path and claim the sword?

3 →	1 →	3 ↓	2 ↓	3 ↓
2 →	4 ↓	3 ↓	1 →	3 ←
2 ↑	2 ↑	🗡	3 ←	1 ↑
2 ↑	2 ↓	3 →	1 ←	4 ←
1 →	2 ↑	2 ↑	3 ↑	1 ←

INTO THE FOREST

Your friends are meeting in the forest. Can you get there without running into the skeleton, creeper, enderman, or witch?

START

TOOLS FOR THE TAKING

Four Minecraft players picked up tools. Who collected what?

To find out, begin at the dot below each player's name and follow it downward. Every time you hit a horizontal line (one that goes across), you must take it. See where each player's path leads, and write each player's name on the space below the correct tool.

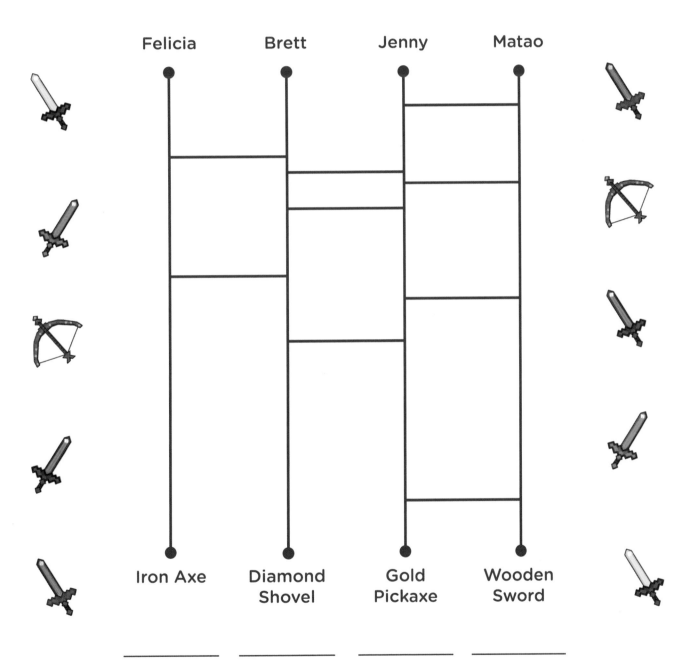

Felicia   Brett   Jenny   Matao

Iron Axe   Diamond Shovel   Gold Pickaxe   Wooden Sword

_____   _____   _____   _____

SAFE SLIMES

In this enchanted maze, you can collect slimes safely if you pick up the blocks in a specific order.

Pick up your first block in the top row (you'll have to guess which one!) and your last block in the bottom row. Collect the blocks in this order:

If you bump into a slime out of order, you're destroyed. Start over. Moving only up, down, left, and right, what path must you take?

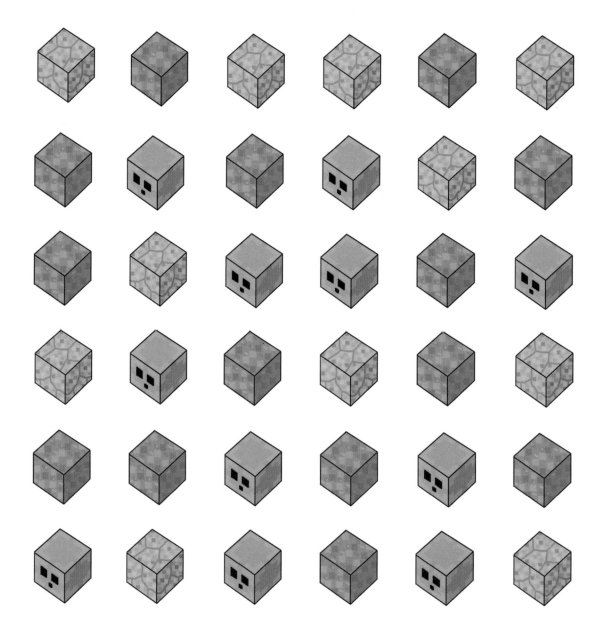

SPELLING BEE #1

Help the bee find its way through this maze to the flowers by spelling 4-letter words.

Make the words by adding MI on the spaces before the given letters. Begin with the word MINE in the top row, and connect the real words until you reach the bottom row. (MIFA is not a real word!)

You can move up, down, left, right, or diagonally.

__FA	MINE	__GO	__BE	__ME	__SO
__OL	__PT	__LK	__LD	__VE	__WN
__AU	__AN	__YO	__CT	__ST	__RD
__SP	__LE	__ND	__LG	__CE	__RT
__LL	__CH	__IZ	__NT	__HY	__OT
__NK	__QO	__PE	__TH	__JU	__UN

FAVORITE THINGS

Follow each player's path, under and over crossing paths, to discover what each likes to do in Minecraft.

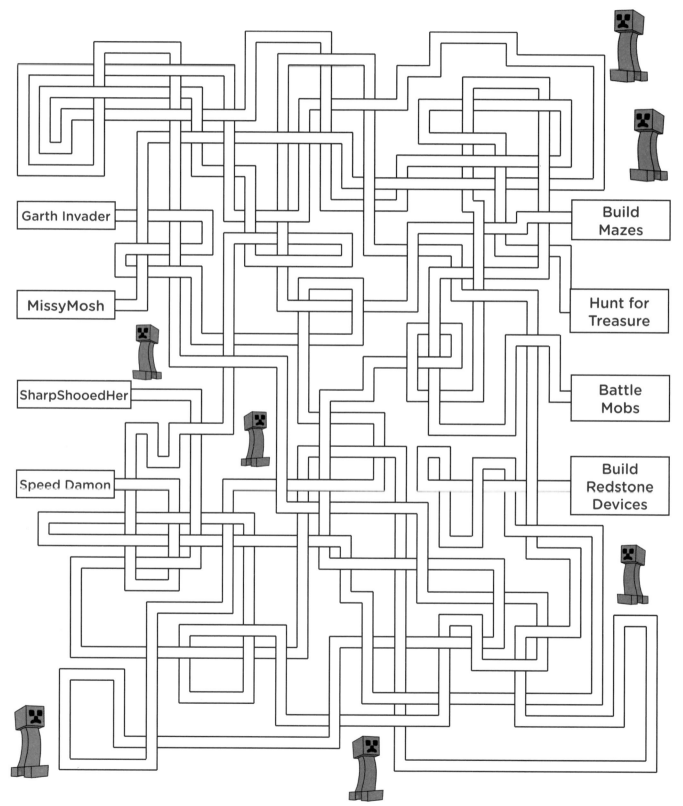

Garth Invader

MissyMosh

SharpShooedHer

Speed Damon

Build Mazes

Hunt for Treasure

Battle Mobs

Build Redstone Devices

EGGCEPTIONAL SPAWNING

Fill the Overworld with mobs of every kind. To do this, draw a line from Start to Finish that passes through every egg once. Your line can go up, down, left, or right, but not diagonally. Get cracking!

Start ←

Finish ←

AROUND THE BLOCKS

Do you know your way around the Minecraft blocks?

Find your way through this maze from START to FINISH. It will be easier if you correctly identify each statement as true or false.

START

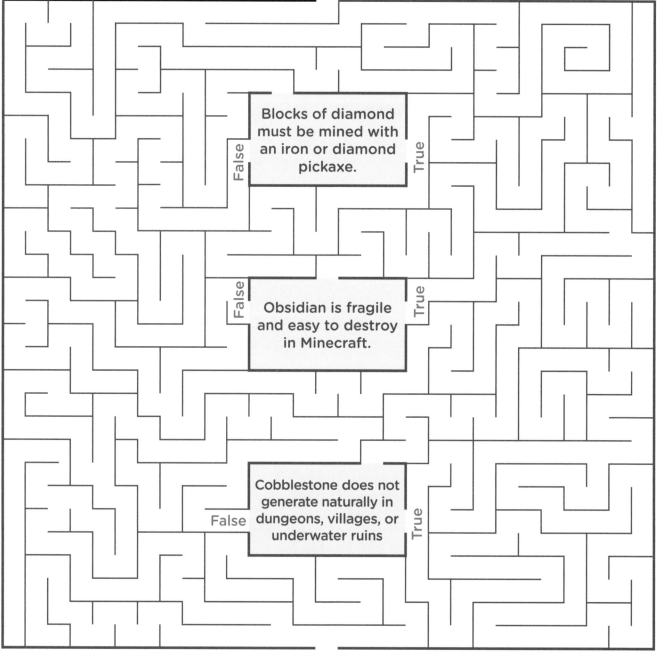

Blocks of diamond must be mined with an iron or diamond pickaxe.

False   True

Obsidian is fragile and easy to destroy in Minecraft.

False   True

Cobblestone does not generate naturally in dungeons, villages, or underwater ruins

False   True

FINISH

HOP TO IT #2

Find your way from the top-left yellow box to the bottom-right yellow box by keeping one icon the same each time you hop boxes. There are two paths to take. See if you pick the right one!

EMERALD FIND

Navigate this maze to find and claim the emeralds.

Begin in a box on the top row (you'll have to guess which one), and follow the numbers and arrows. Each square tells you how many spaces to move and in what direction. Arrows leading off the grid are dead ends.

Can you find the path to the gems?

2↓	4→	3↓	3↓	4↓
2→	3↓	1↓	3←	1↑
2↓	3→	2←	2←	1↓
1→	2↑	2↓	1↑	4←
4↑	1→	💎	3↑	1←

TEMPLE ESCAPE

You are trapped in a desert temple. Can you find your way out?

FINISH

START

RUN!

Four Minecraft players are being chased by mobs. Who is being chased by what? To find out, begin at the dot below each mob and follow it downward. Every time you hit a horizontal line (one that goes across), you must take it.

See where each mob's path leads, and write the name of the mob below the person it's chasing.

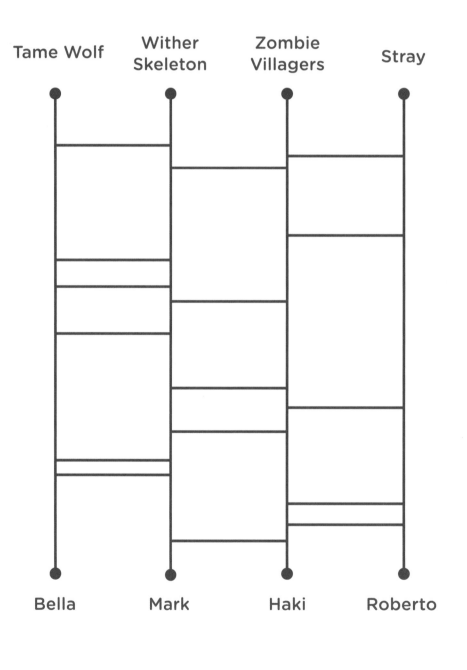

Tame Wolf   Wither Skeleton   Zombie Villagers   Stray

Bella   Mark   Haki   Roberto

_____   _____   _____   _____

SPECIMEN COLLECTION

You are collecting specimens for a new aquatic biome. You need: dolphins, squid, and turtles, but they must be collected in this order.

Pick up your first dolphin in the top row and your last turtle in the bottom row. Moving only up, down, left, and right, what path must you take?

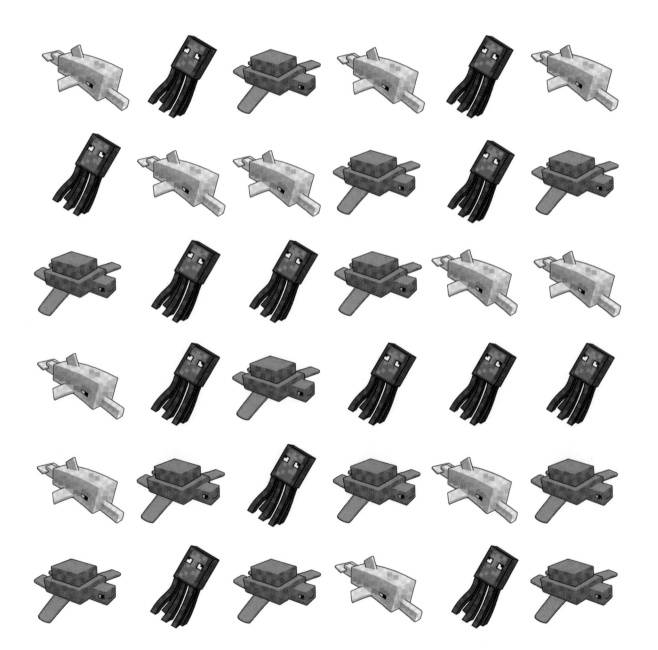

19

SPELLING BEE #2

Help the bee find its way through this maze to the flowers by spelling 4-letter words.

Make the words by adding M to the first space and N to the second space in the given letters. Begin with the word MINE in the top row, and connect the real words until you reach the bottom row. (MINZ is not a real word!)

You can move up, down, left, right, or diagonally.

_ O _ T	_ E _ G	_ S _ A	_ I _ Z	M I N E	_ U _ L
_ I _ O	_ A _ W	_ Z _ K	_ E _ D	_ O _ D	_ A _ F
_ R _ O	_ Y _ A	_ U _ R	_ O _ K	_ I _ H	_ E _ B
_ I _ X	_ P _ E	_ A _ Y	_ J _ I	_ E _ K	_ O _ O
_ A _ Q	_ O _ Z	_ E _ U	_ Y _ V	_ U _ N	_ A _ T
_ U _ F	_ I _ T	_ W _ O	_ A _ V	_ E _ K	_ U _ P

CHEST QUEST

Six Minecraft players are trying to find an enchanted chest. Follow each player's path, under and over crossing paths, to discover which players, if any, find it.

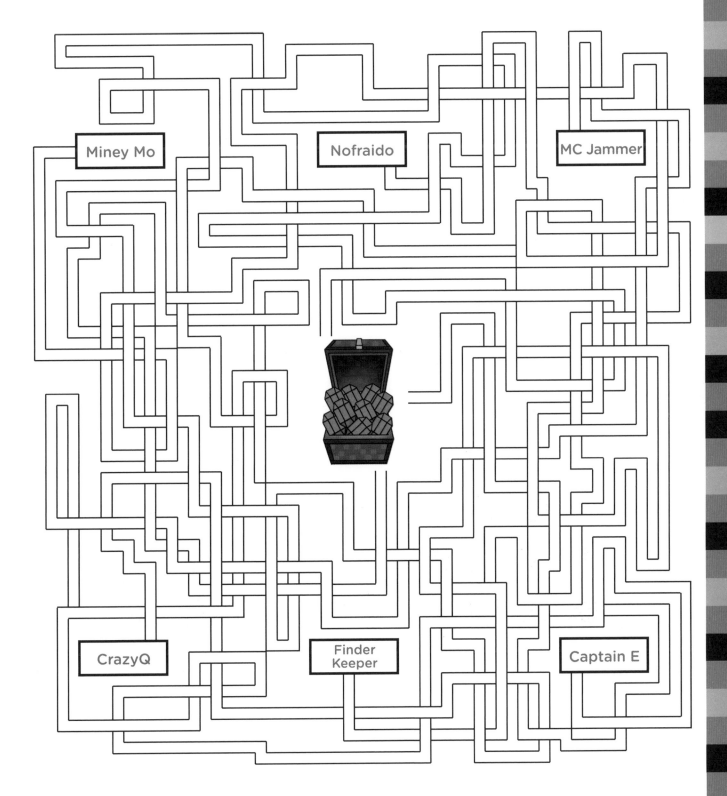

FROG FITNESS

Help the frog hop to safety. Draw a line from Start to Finish that includes each and every lily pad in the pond. Your line can go up, down, left, or right, but not diagonally. Get hopping!

Start

Finish

ENCHANTÉ

Find your way through this enchanting maze from START to FINISH. It will be easier if you correctly identify each statement as true or false.

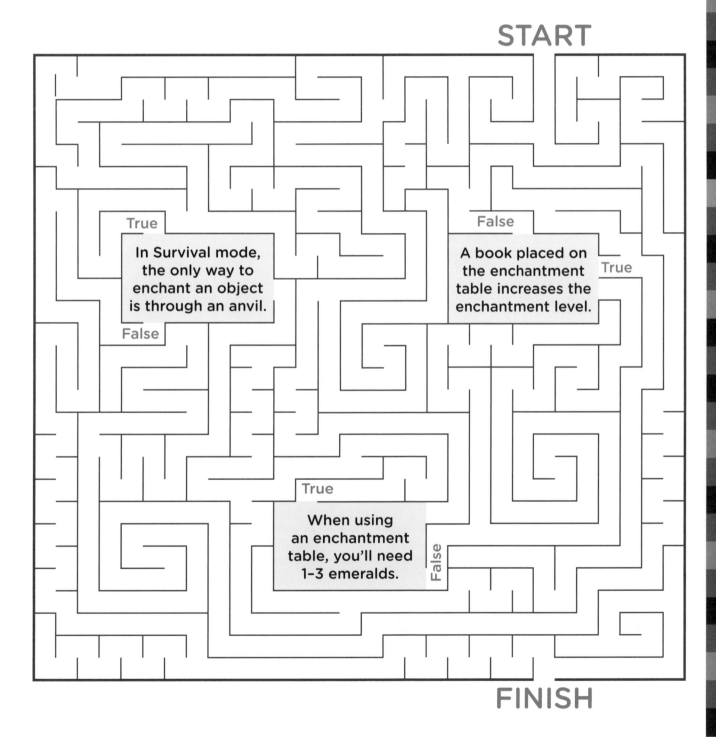

START

True

In Survival mode, the only way to enchant an object is through an anvil.

False

False

A book placed on the enchantment table increases the enchantment level.

True

True

When using an enchantment table, you'll need 1–3 emeralds.

False

FINISH

HOP TO IT #3

Find your way from the top-left yellow box to the bottom-right yellow box by keeping one icon the same each time you hop boxes. There are several paths to take. See if you can find the right one!

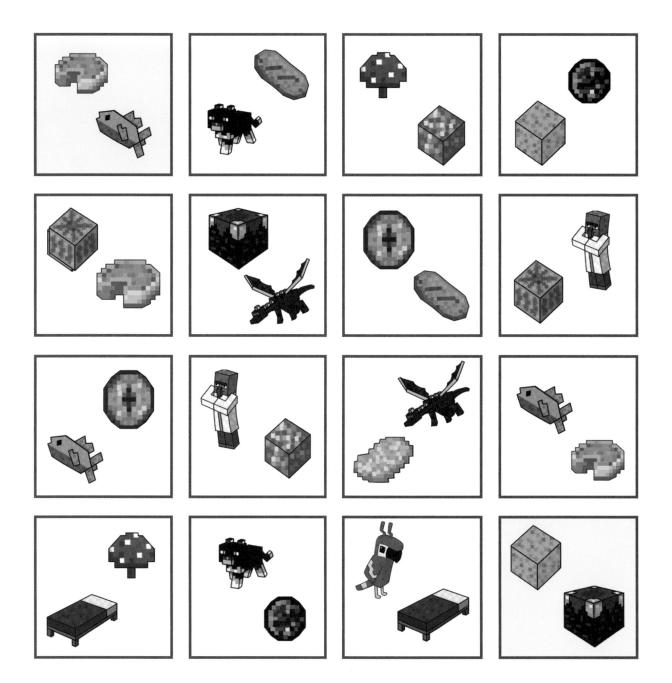

NAP TIME

Help the cat find the path to the warm furnace (where he will sit and nap until you feed him a fish).

Begin in one of the four boxes to the right of, or below, the cat (you'll have to guess which one), and follow the numbers and arrows. Each square tells you how many spaces to move and in what direction. Arrows leading off the grid are dead ends.

		3 ↓	5 ↓	3 ↓	1 ←	5 ↓	4 ←
		3 ↓	3 →	3 ←	3 ↓	1 ↑	3 ←
4 →	4 ↓	5 ↓	5 ↓	4 ↓	1 ↓	4 ←	1 ↑
7 →	1 ↓	1 →	2 ↑	3 ←	3 →	6 ←	3 ↑
1 ↑	5 →	2 ←	2 ↓	1 ←	2 ↑	2 ↑	2 ↓
4 →	2 ↓	5 →	2 →	4 ↓	4 ↑	5 ←	3 ↑
1 ↑	4 →	1 ↑	3 ←	2 ←	6 ↑		
6 →	2 →	2 ←	1 →	3 ↑	1 →		

DIAMOND DASH

This room is full of creepers. Can you dash in, grab the diamonds, and get out without . . . you know . . . getting blown up?

START   STOP

GOOD TRADES BAD TRADE

Five Minecraft players are trading with villagers. One is silly enough to try and trade with a nitwit.

Begin at the dot below each player's name and follow it downward. Every time you hit a horizontal line (one that goes across), you must take it. See where each player's path leads, and write each player's name below the correct trader on the line.

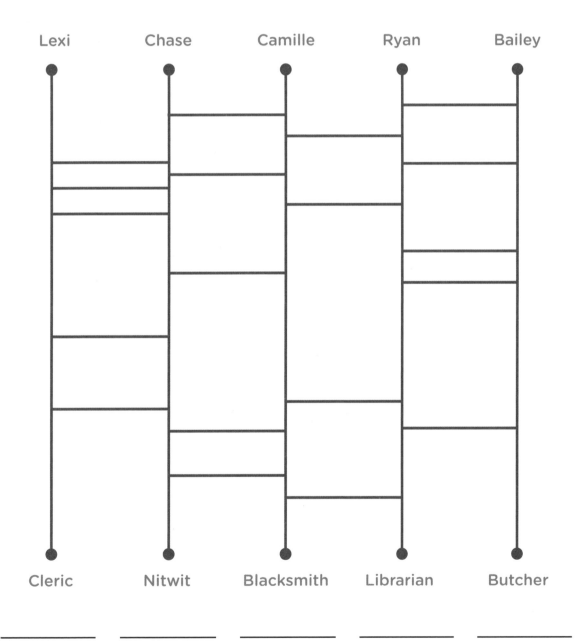

Lexi	Chase	Camille	Ryan	Bailey

Cleric	Nitwit	Blacksmith	Librarian	Butcher

SMOOTHIES FOR SIX

You are making smoothies for six friends. For each smoothie, you need to add the following ingredients, in this order, to a blender:

Gather your ingredients below. You must pick up your first apple in the top row and your last watermelon slice in the bottom row.

Moving only up, down, left, and right, what path must you take to get all the ingredients for six smoothies?

SPELLING BEE #3

Help the bee find its way through this maze to the flowers by spelling 4-letter words.

Make the words by adding NE after the given letters. Begin with the word MINE in the top row, and connect the real words until you reach the bottom row. (CRNE is not a real word!)

You can move up, down, left, right, or diagonally.

MINE	BU__	JE__	EA__	SC__	FI__	JE__	CR__
AT__	HE__	BR__	CR__	LO__	ST__	DO__	VI__
LA__	ZO__	MA__	DU__	IF__	UR__	SA__	FO__
GU__	CH__	MO__	GR__	OI__	FA__	TU__	OP__
OU__	HO__	NI__	QU__	MS__	BO__	RE__	LI__
DI__	KY__	EG__	EA__	CA__	PL__	AJ__	TO__
BL__	PI__	WU__	DR__	UR__	NO__	KR__	BR__
NE__	CO__	AU__	JU__	GO__	FE__	CL__	HU__

29

INTO BATTLE

Four Minecraft players are heading into battle with hostile mobs. Follow each player's path, under and over crossing paths, to discover who's fighting whom.

Ghast

Drowned

Scarrr	Clash
Jaction	Attax

Shulker

Evoker

CACTUS CROP COLLECTION

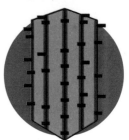

You've been growing cacti so you can build traps, and your cactus crop is ready to harvest.

To do this, draw a line from Start to Finish that passes through every cactus once. Your line can go up, down, left, or right, but not diagonally. Careful! Don't get stuck!

Finish   Start

LAVA KNOWLEDGE

A little bit of lava knowledge will help you out here.

Find your way through this maze from START to FINISH. It will be easier if you correctly identify each statement as true or false.

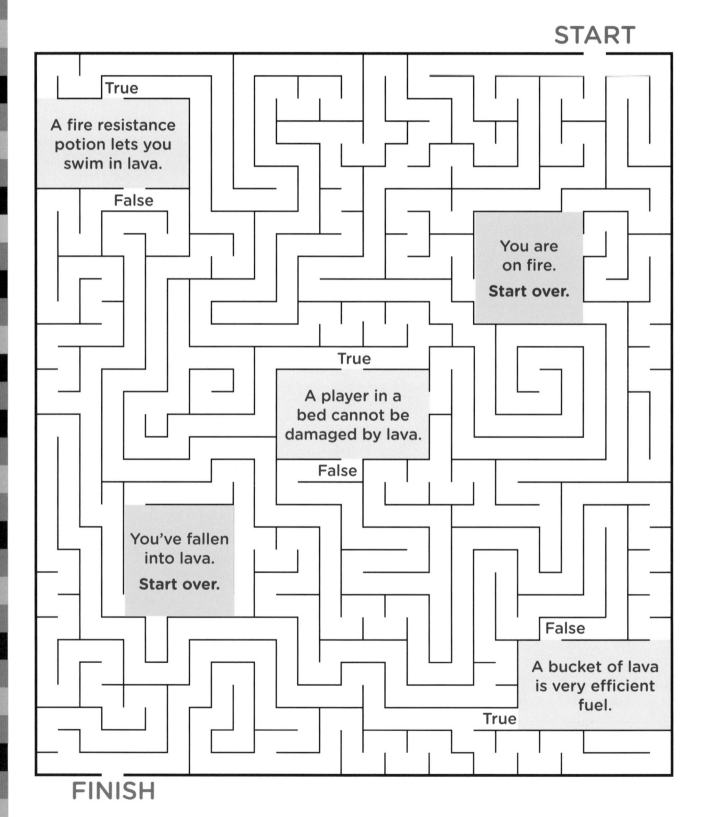

START

True

A fire resistance potion lets you swim in lava.

False

You are on fire.

Start over.

True

A player in a bed cannot be damaged by lava.

False

You've fallen into lava.

Start over.

False

A bucket of lava is very efficient fuel.

True

FINISH

HOP TO IT #4

Find your way from the top-left yellow box to the bottom-right yellow box by keeping one icon the same each time you hop boxes. There are two paths to take. See if you can find the right one!

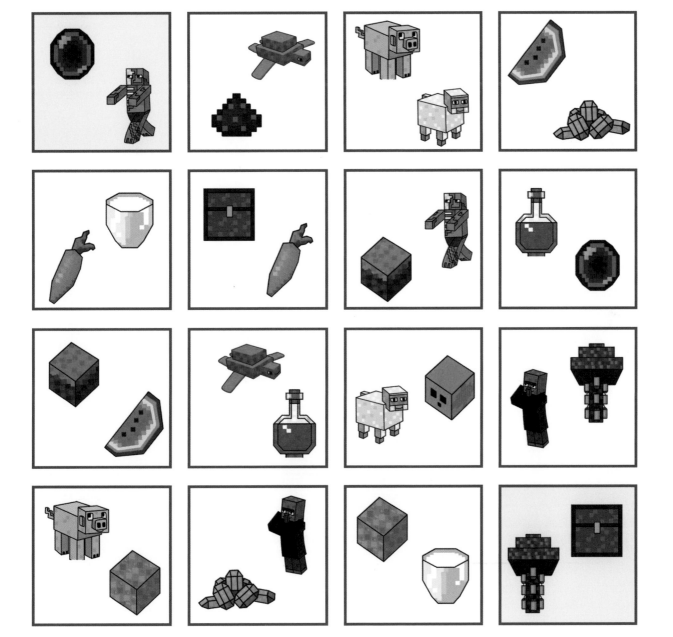

LOST BEACON

Steve needs to get to the beacon to gain power, but an unbreakable barrier stands between him and the beacon. He can only access it by following this tricky maze.

Begin in one of the four boxes above, below, or to the left of Steve (it's up to you to figure it out) and follow the numbers and arrows. Each square tells you how many spaces to move and in what direction. Arrows leading off the grid are dead ends.

Can you help Steve find the path to the beacon?

6→	7→	2↓	4←	3↓	2→	3↑	4↓
7→	3→	3↑	5→	1↓	1→	6↓	2↓
2↑	1←	4↓	4→	2↑	3↓	1←	4↓
2↑	1←	3↑			4↓	1←	2↓
2↓	4↓	2←			3↑	2←	2←
2↓	4↑	1←	3→	3→	5←	2↑	3←
5→	3↑	4→	1↓	3←	6↑	4↑	4←
7→	5↑	2↑	2←	1↑	1←	4←	6↑

AN ENCHANTED HOE

If you pick up the gold ingots and sticks before exiting this maze, you can craft a hoe that's enchanted with Unbreaking and Mending.

Can you collect all four items and find your way out of the maze?

START

Congratulations! You've earned two enchantments for your new golden hoe. **Yes** ← **Did you collect all four items?** **No** → Try again!

A VERY SMART PIG
(AND A FUNNY GIRL)

Find your way through this maze to discover the answer to Steve's question below. Follow the lines to determine which letter goes on each numbered line.

Begin at the dot below each number and follow it downward. Every time you hit a horizontal line (one that goes across), you must take it. See what letter each number connects with.

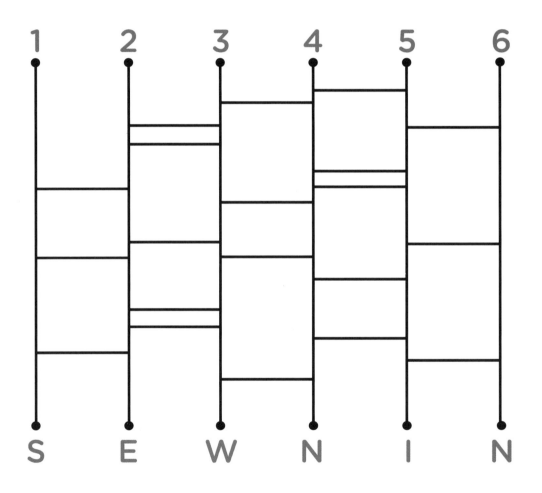

1   2   3   4   5   6

S   E   W   N   I   N

Alex: I have the smartest pig in Minecraft.

Steve: What's its name?

Alex: __ __ __ __ __ __ __ __
        3 6 4 2 1 6 5 3

MAIN COURSE MIX-UP

You are collecting a week's worth of meat from the village butcher.

You must pick up your first chicken drumstick in the top row and your last rabbit stew in the bottom row.

Moving only up, down, left, and right, what path must you take?

SPELLING BEE #4

Help the bee find its way through this maze to the flowers by spelling 4-letter words.
Make the words by adding IN between the given letters.
Begin with the word MINE in the top row, and connect the real words until you reach the bottom row. (HINR is not a real word!)
You can move up, down, left, right, or diagonally.

L__D	R__K	W__P	F__G	M<u>IN</u>E	H__R	L__K	Z__G
G__D	L__T	N__D	W__G	K__T	N__E	B__T	S__Y
V__E	C__G	S__K	L__X	F__T	P__D	E__G	R__D
R__G	H__O	B__Y	J__T	L__P	T__Y	M__R	S__K
N__W	F__D	I__G	S__G	P__K	Z__T	B__D	G__G
W__K	H__L	P__E	A__W	D__F	T__C	P__T	T__T
F__E	Z__C	G__Z	F__Y	H__T	W__D	S__T	O__K
L__F	R__P	U__T	K__G	V__G	Y__U	M__B	K__Z

A SECRET MESSAGE

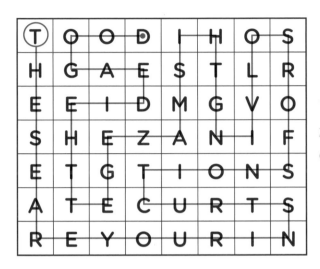

T	O	O	D	I	H	O	S
H	G	A	E	S	T	L	R
E	E	I	D	M	G	V	O
S	H	E	Z	A	N	I	F
E	T	G	T	I	O	N	S
A	T	E	C	U	R	T	S
R	E	Y	O	U	R	I	N

These are your instructions for solving this maze. Get the idea? Good!

P	L	E	H	N	A	L	U
Y	U	Z	B	D	C	F	F
O	P	Z	E	N	I	R	Y
U	E	L	I	F	M	A	A
S	V	E	N	O	E	M	L
O	L	S	G	I	N	A	P

_____ __ _ _____ _____ __ ____ ___

____ ___ _____ _____.

BEDS WANTED!

Four Minecraft players have not had their avatars go to bed for over six in-game days, and phantoms are prowling. They are all trying to get through this maze to a bed. Follow each player's path, under and over crossing paths, to discover which players, if any, find a bed. Who is finally getting some rest?

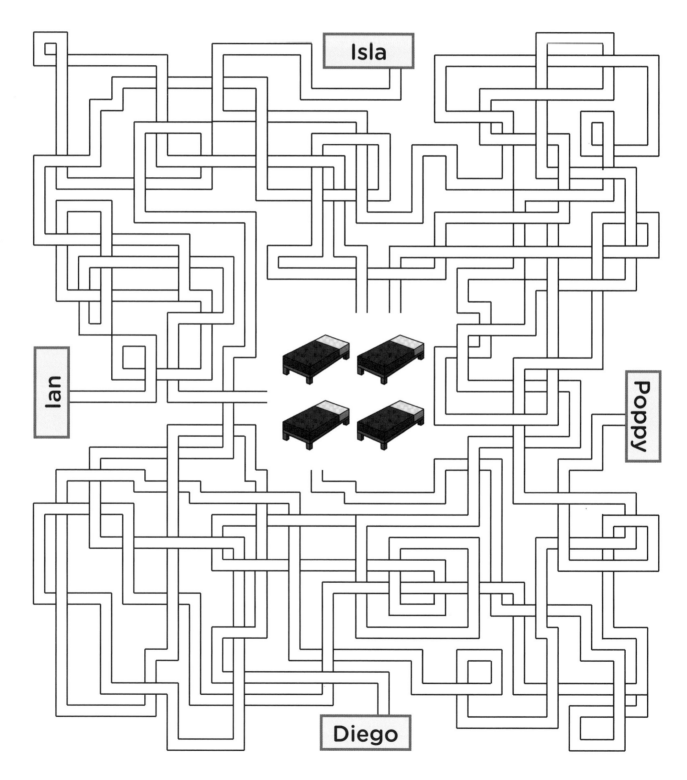

COBWEB DREAMS

A Minecrafter calling himself SpiderGuy dreams of building a mansion out of cobwebs. Help him collect all the cobwebs below.

To do this, draw a line from Start to Finish that includes each and every cobweb once. Your line can go up, down, left, or right, but not diagonally.

Start

Finish

SADDLE UP!

Find your way through this maze from START to FINISH. It will be easier if you correctly identify each statement as true or false.

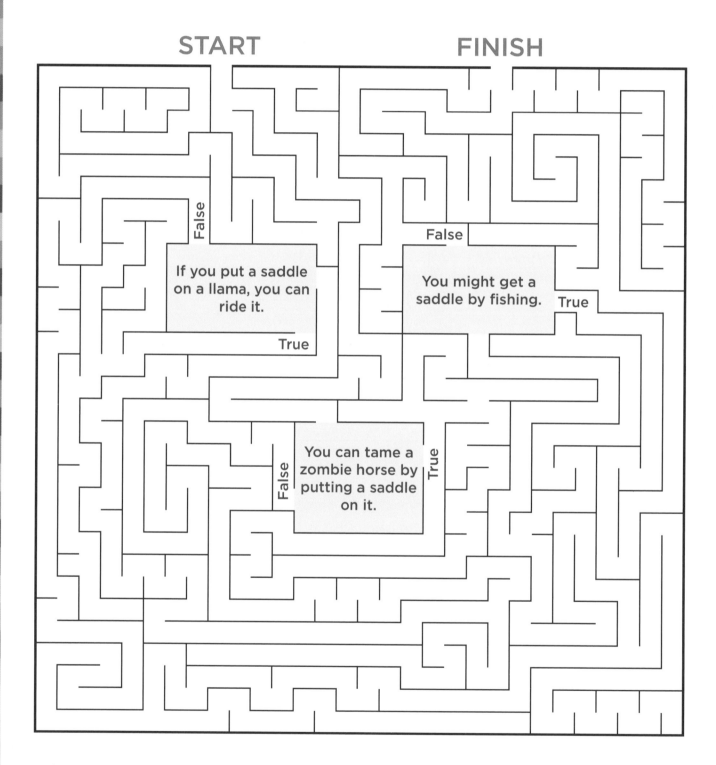

False

If you put a saddle on a llama, you can ride it.

True

False

You might get a saddle by fishing.

True

You can tame a zombie horse by putting a saddle on it.

False

True

HOP TO IT #5

Find your way from the top-left yellow box to the bottom-right yellow box by keeping one icon the same each time you hop boxes. There are several paths to take. See if you can find the right one!

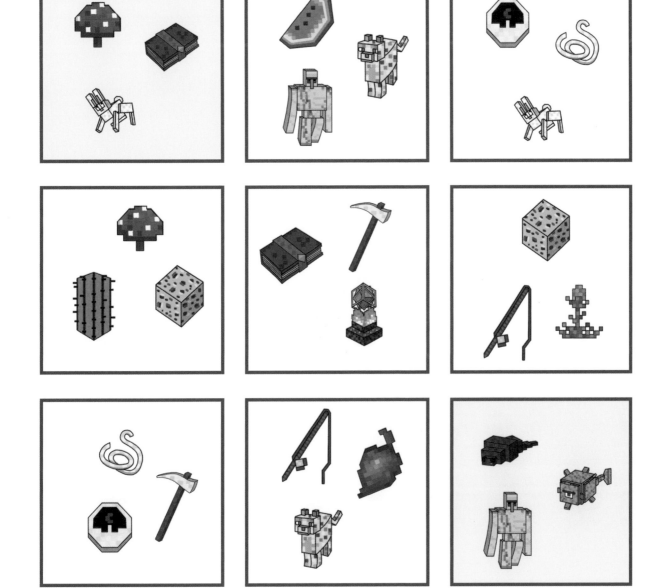

THE PEARLY PATH

Find the path to the Ender pearl and it is yours.

Begin in one of the four corner boxes (you'll have to guess which one), and follow the numbers and arrows. Each square tells you how many spaces to move and in what direction. Arrows leading off the grid are dead ends.

Can you find the path to the Ender pearl? Choose a corner and begin!

3 ↓	4 →	2 →	2 ↓	1 ←	4 ↓	3 ↓
3 ↓	5 →	2 →	5 ↓	1 ↓	5 ←	3 ←
6 →	3 ↓	3 ←	2 →	3 ←	2 →	2 ↓
2 →	3 ↑	3 ↓	🔵	3 ←	2 ↓	1 ←
1 →	4 ↑	3 ↑	1 ↑	1 ←	4 ←	4 ←
3 →	3 →	5 ↑	2 ↑	4 ←	3 ←	2 →
4 ↑	5 ↑	3 →	1 →	3 ↑	5 ↑	5 ←

MOB HOUSE

Try to make your way through this mob house without running into any mobs as you go.

START

FINISH

SCAVENGER HUNT FINDS

Five Minecraft players have found between 1 and 5 objects for a scavenger hunt. How many has each player found?

To find out, begin at the dot below each player's name and follow it downward. Every time you hit a horizontal line (one that goes across), you must take it. See where each player's path leads, and write each name below the correct number. Who found the most?

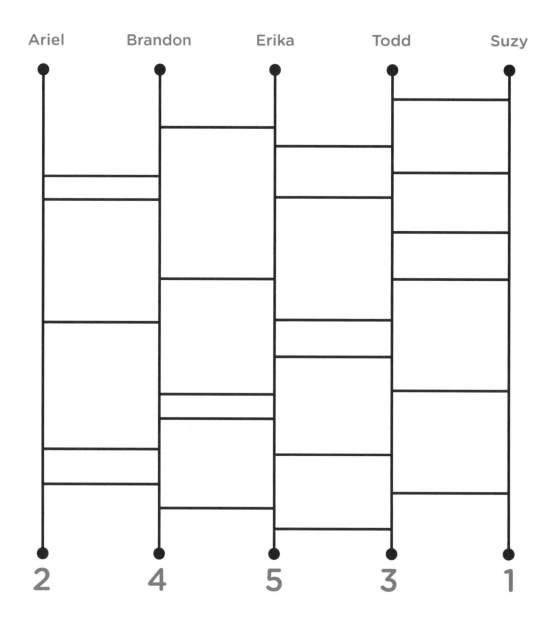

Ariel	Brandon	Erika	Todd	Suzy

2	4	5	3	1

MOOSHROOM SHEARING

It's time to shear the mooshrooms. You must pick up the first set of shears in the top row and wind up with your last cow on the bottom row. To get there, you must move from shears to mooshroom to cow, in that order, until you exit the herd at the bottom row.

Moving only up, down, left, and right, what path must you take?

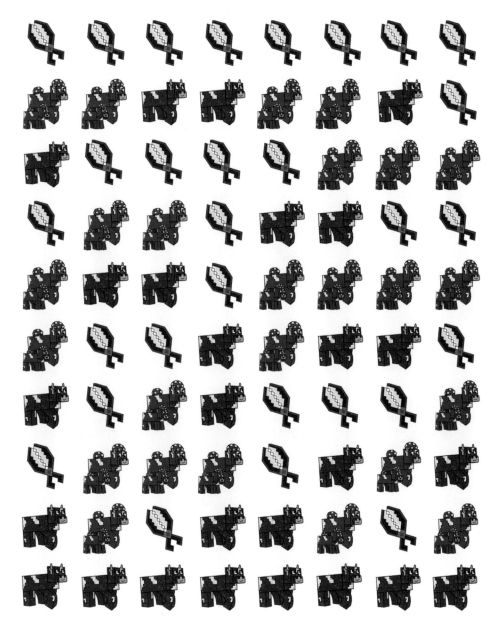

SPELLING BEE #5

Help the bee find its way through this maze to the flowers by spelling 4-letter words.

Make the words by adding M before the given letters and E after the given letters. Begin with the word MINE in the top row, and connect the real words until you reach the bottom row. (MUDE is not a real word!)

You can move up, down, left, right, or diagonally.

MINE	_AL_	_UD_	_IK_	_AB_	_OC_	_IY_	_OZ_
_OR_	_OG_	_AF_	_AC_	_UH_	_IL_	_OI_	_EH_
_IJ_	_IM_	_UK_	_AU_	_OV_	_UM_	_AD_	_YL_
_TL_	_SN_	_US_	_AK_	_OM_	_EO_	_IP_	_UT_
_AT_	_LL_	_UQ_	_EL_	_IS_	_OT_	_UU_	_IC_
_IV_	_IK_	_AN_	_OW_	_UL_	_OD_	_OP_	_AX_
_OZ_	_PR_	_UP_	_AR_	_AY_	_RT_	_IB_	_AI_
_UW_	_OL_	_CH_	_EV_	_AZ_	_AE_	_ID_	_OB_

WHERE AM I?

Four Minecraft players wandered into new biomes. Follow each player's path, under and over crossing paths, to discover where each is now.

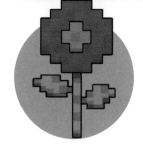

Swamp

Deep Ocean

Ambler

Drifter

Gad2222

Journey-Man

Arctic

Jungle

'NOTHER NETHER STAR, PLEASE

Let's face it: Nether stars aren't easy to get in Minecraft. But you can collect a whole bunch here.

To do it, draw a line from Start to Finish that passes through every Nether star once. Your line can go up, down, left, or right, but not diagonally. On your mark, get set, collect!

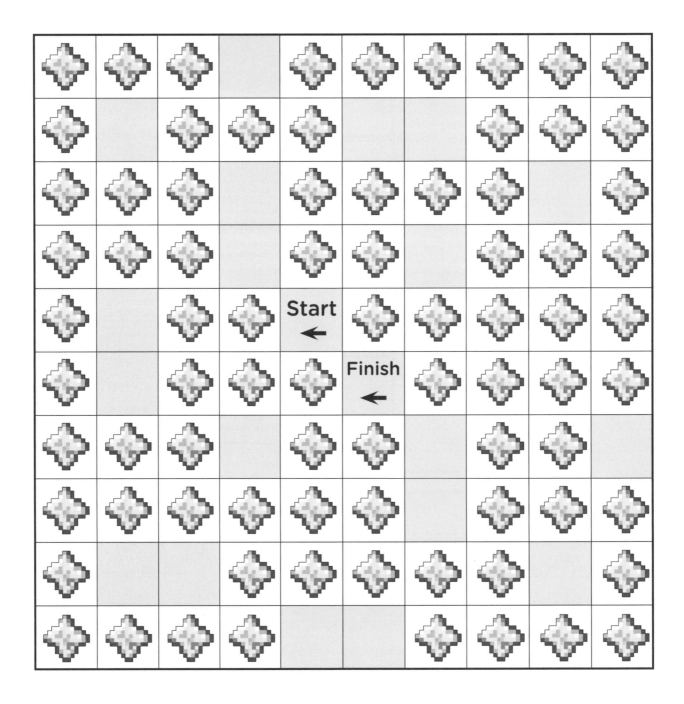

CHEST JESTS

Chests can be funny things . . .

Find your way through this maze from START to FINISH.
It will be easier if you correctly identify each statement as
true or false.

START

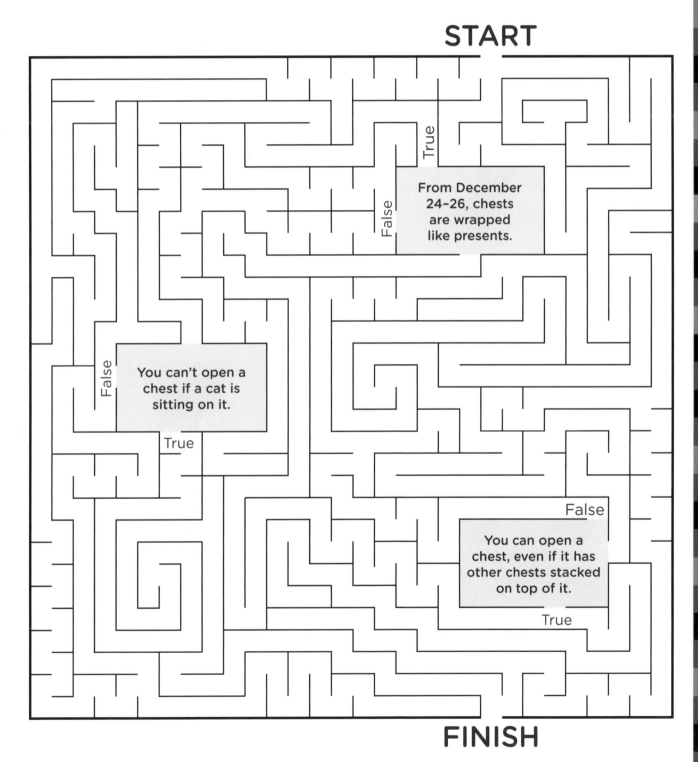

True

False

From December
24–26, chests
are wrapped
like presents.

False

You can't open a
chest if a cat is
sitting on it.

True

False

You can open a
chest, even if it has
other chests stacked
on top of it.

True

FINISH

HOP TO IT #6

Find your way from the top-left yellow box to the bottom-right yellow box by keeping one icon the same each time you hop boxes. There are several paths to take. See if you can find the right one!

52

QUICK! YOU CAN SAVE US ALL!

Uh-oh. A TNT block will explode if you don't get to the center of this maze and flip the switch.

Begin in one of the four corner boxes (you'll have to guess which one), and follow the numbers and arrows. Each square tells you how many spaces to move and in what direction. Arrows leading off the grid are dead ends.

Can you find the path to the lever so you can flip it and prevent the TNT from exploding?

3 →	8 ↓	4 ↓	6 ↓	2 ↓	1 ←	8 ↓	2 ↑	5 ↓
7 →	3 ↓	2 ↓	2 ←	2 ↓	5 ←	6 ↓	2 ↓	6 ←
2 ↑	4 ↓	2 ←	1 →	3 →	4 ←	1 ↓	5 ↓	2 ←
1 ←	7 →	3 →	4 ↓	1 ↓	6 ←	3 ←	3 ↓	7 ←
4 →	1 ↑	2 ←	3 ←		4 ↑	2 ←	3 ←	3 ←
5 ↑	2 ↓	2 →	1 →	2 ↓	1 →	5 ↑	3 →	7 ←
2 →	4 →	1 ↑	5 →	2 ↑	4 ↑	4 ↓	2 ↓	4 ↑
1 ↑	4 →	5 ↑	1 ←	4 →	6 ↑	1 ↑	7 ←	6 ↑
5 →	2 ↑	8 ↑	7 ↑	4 ↑	3 ↑	3 ←	5 ←	4 ↑

GO FOR GLOW

Can you find your way through this Nether maze to get to the glowstone? If you fall in the lava, go back to START and try again.

FINISH

START

LAUGH LINES

Follow the lines in the maze to determine which letter goes on each numbered line. If you follow the maze correctly, you'll find the answer to the joke.

Begin at the dot below each letter and follow it downward.
Every time you hit a horizontal line (one that goes across), you must take it. See what number each letter connects with, and write that letter on the correct space.

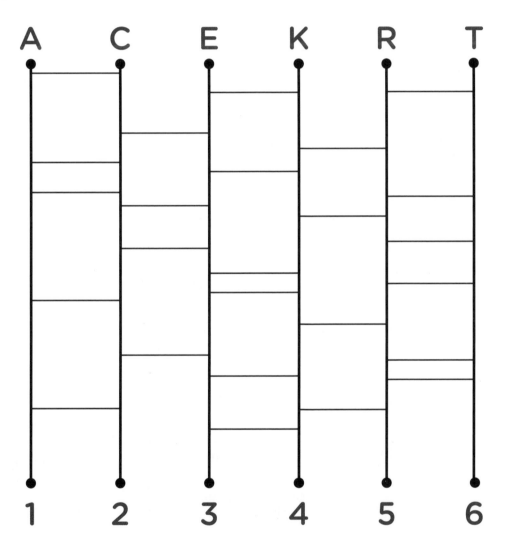

A   C   E   K   R   T

1   2   3   4   5   6

What's another name for a gold ingot?

__ __ __   __ __   __ __ __ __
2   4   3   1 4   5   4   2   6

MOB SCHOOL CARPOOL

It's your turn to drive the mobs to school. You must pick up all 16 mobs in a specific order or they will get mad and attack. You must pick up your first blaze in the top row and your last zombie pigman in the bottom row, and you must pick them up in this order:

Moving only up, down, left, and right, what path must you take?

SPELLING BEE #6

Help the bee find its way through this maze to the flowers by spelling 4-letter words.

Make the words by adding I on the first space and E on the second space in each letter set. Begin with the word MINE in the top row, and connect the real words until you reach the bottom row. (ZIGE is not a real word!)

You can move up, down, left, right, or diagonally.

B_P_	S_B_	P_L_	R_P_	S_F_	F_D_	M**I**N**E**	Z_G_
J_B_	P_M_	K_B_	C_C_	W_G_	L_M_	T_G_	F_N_
D_D_	H_R_	R_R_	Y_D_	P_P_	G_M_	S_Q_	K_L_
W_B_	H_V_	P_T_	Z_P_	W_S_	A_P_	T_D_	Q_T_
C_T_	O_N_	K_T_	F_B_	U_P_	F_V_	E_J_	H_K_
A_B_	C_M_	D_C_	W_R_	R_H_	Z_M_	Y_D_	N_C_
G_X_	T_M_	F_Y_	H_Q_	B_T_	G_V_	S_D_	J_M_
N_R_	W_G_	L_K_	S_C_	C_H_	T_F_	G_H_	C_E

CHICKEN HERDING

Uh-oh! The chickens have escaped from your farm, and now you must round them up. To do this, draw a line from Start to Finish that passes through every chicken once. Your line can go up, down, left, or right, but not diagonally. On your mark, get set . . . "Heeeeere, chicken-chicken-chicken!"

Start

Finish

SHEDDING LIGHT ON REDSTONE TORCHES

Knowledge of redstone torches can illuminate the correct path here. Don't worry, though. If you're not up on redstone torches, you can feel your way.

Find your way through this maze from START to FINISH. It will be easier if you correctly identify each statement as true or false.

START

FINISH

True

Redstone torches can be found in igloos.

False

Redstone torches can only be attached to the bottom of a transparent block.

True

False

True

A redstone torch always affects the block it is attached to.

False

HOP TO IT #7

Find your way from the top-left yellow box to the lower-right yellow box by keeping one icon the same each time you hop boxes. There are several paths to take. See if you can find the right one!

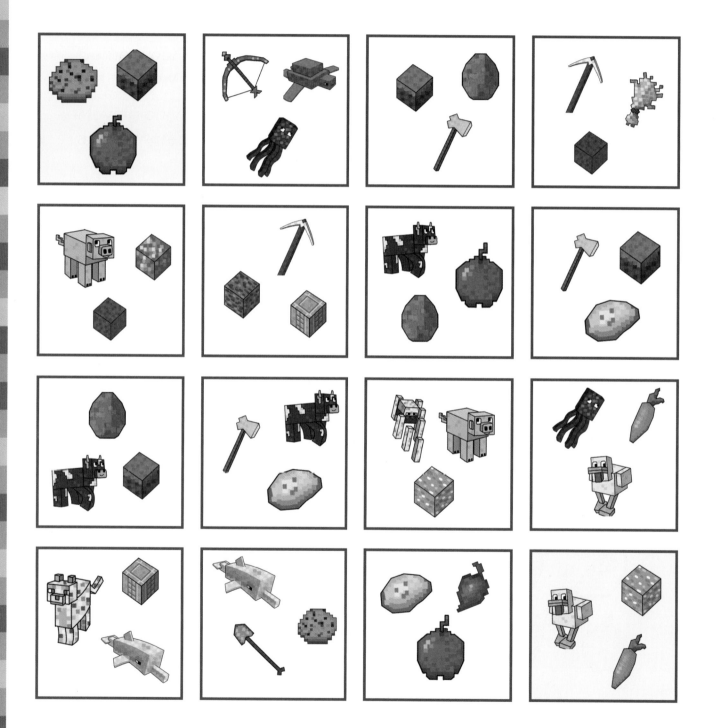

GO FOR THE GOLD

Make your way to the golden hoe so you can enchant it with Unbreaking.

Begin in one of the four corner boxes (you'll have to guess which one), and follow the numbers and arrows. Each square tells you how many spaces to move and in what direction. Arrows leading off the grid are dead ends.

Can you find the path to the hoe?

4 ↓	3 ↓	6 ↓	4 ←	3 ←	2 ←	5 ↓
5 →	1 ←	1 ↑	1 ↓	1 ←	4 ↓	4 ←
5 →	5 →	1 ↓	1 →	1 ↑	2 ↓	1 ↓
2 ↓	3 →	2 ←	🪓	2 ↑	3 ↑	1 ←
4 →	2 →	4 →	1 ↑	4 ↑	1 →	3 ↑
4 →	3 ↑	3 ↑	2 ←	1 ↓	3 ←	3 ←
4 ↑	5 ↑	1 →	2 ↑	1 →	5 ↑	5 ←

PURSUING PRISMARINE

Can you avoid the drowned and the guardian to reach the prismarine in the ocean monument? Give it a shot!

START

UNDEAD HUMOR

Uncover the answer to the joke by following the lines in the maze to determine which letter goes on each numbered line.

Begin at the dot below each letter and follow it downward.

Every time you hit a horizontal line (one that goes across), you must take it. See what number each letter connects with, then write that letter on the space with that number.

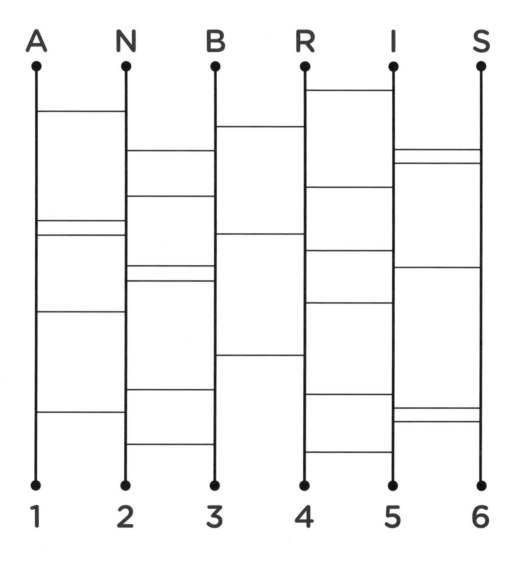

A N B R I S

1 2 3 4 5 6

What did the zombie order for dinner?

___ ___ ___ ___ ___ ___!
5   4   3   6   2   1

EGG HUNT

You are collecting two dozen spawn eggs. It's delicate work. If you don't do it correctly, the mobs will hatch and attack you!

You must pick up your first egg in the top row and your last egg in the bottom row, and you must pick them up in this order:

Moving only up, down, left, and right, what path must you take?

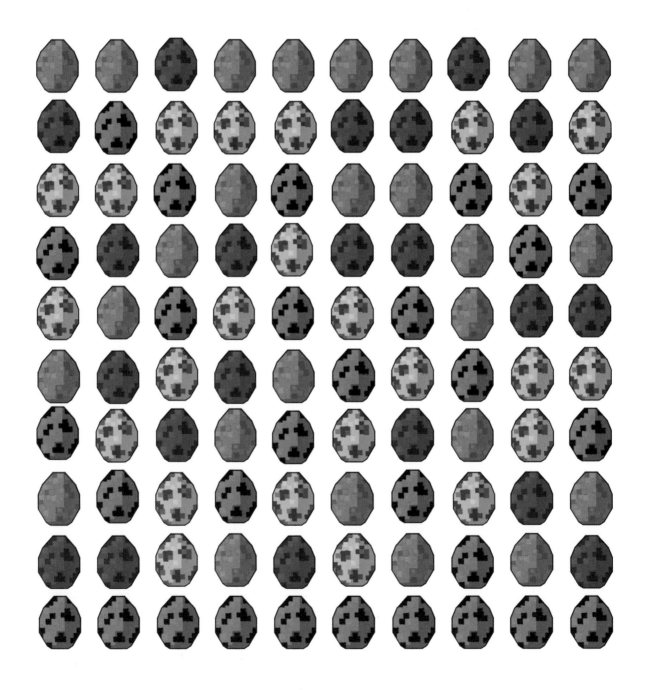

SPELLING BEE #7

Help the bee find its way through this maze to the flowers by spelling 5-letter words.

Make the words by adding CR before the given letters. Begin with the word CRAFT in the top row, and connect the real words until you reach the bottom row. (CRONG is not a real word!)

You can move up, down, left, right, or diagonally.

CRAFT	__OWD	__IDE	__UMP	__ESP	__YPT	__EPE	__ALK
__IMP	__ONG	__ASH	__OSH	__ESS	__USE	__EAT	__OON
__UDE	__ITE	__UMB	__ALM	__UGE	__ANE	__OLE	__AIL
__UEL	__OUG	__IFT	__EST	__EWL	__USH	__ISP	__EAN
__UST	__ACE	__IME	__ANG	__ODA	__ATE	__UBE	_ACK
__EEP	__PLE	__YNG	__AWL	__EAM	__ILF	__OPT	__EEK
__OLY	__EDO	__IFY	__OAP	__IGE	__IFE	__AVE	__ANK
__ELT	__UFF	__SPY	__ILL	__AZE	__OWN	__GST	__LPY

ANSWERS

PAGE 3,
CAVE EXPLORERS

Carlos, Cara, and Camilo find the cave. Cami
does not.

PAGE 4,
REDSTONE ROUNDUP

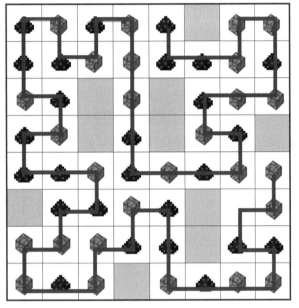

PAGE 5,
A DOG'S LIFE

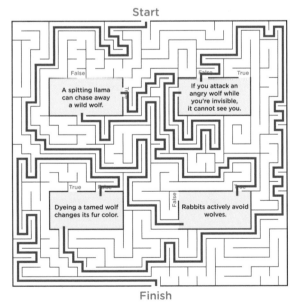

PAGE 6,
HOP TO IT #1

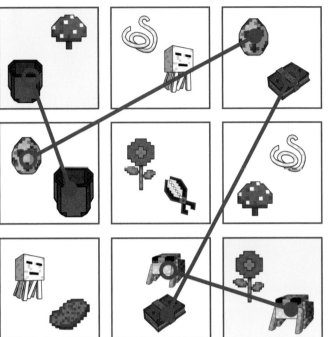

PAGE 7,
CAPTURE THE SWORD

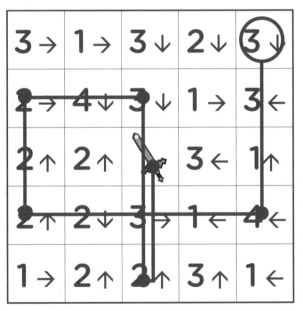

PAGE 8,
INTO THE FOREST

START

PAGE 9,
TOOLS FOR THE TAKING

Felicia - Diamond Shovel
Brett - Wooden Sword
Jenny - Iron Axe
Matao - Gold Pickaxe

PAGE 10,
SAFE SLIMES

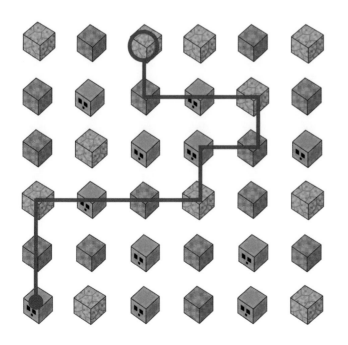

PAGE 11,
SPELLING BEE #1

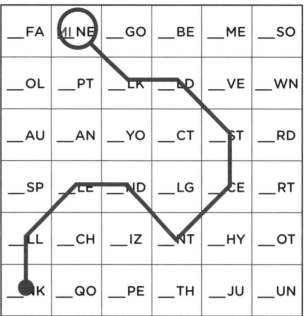

PAGE 12,
FAVORITE THINGS

Garth Invader - Battle Mobs
MissyMosh - Build Redstone Devices
SharpShooedHer - Build Mazes
Speed Damon - Hunt for Treasure

PAGE 13,
EGGCEPTIONAL HARVEST

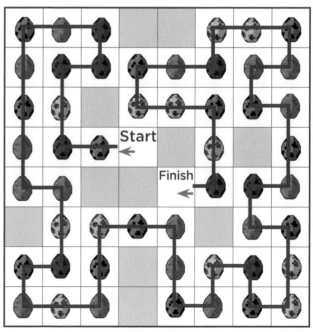

PAGE 14,
AROUND THE BLOCKS

START

FINISH

PAGE 16,
EMERALD FIND

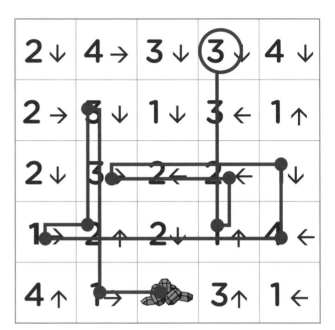

PAGE 15,
HOP TO IT #2

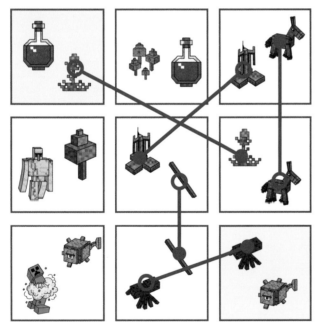

PAGE 17,
TEMPLE ESCAPE

FINISH!

START

PAGE 18,
RUN!

Tame wolf - Haki
Wither skeleton - Roberto
Zombie villagers - Bella
Stray - Mark

PAGE 19,
SPECIMEN COLLECTION

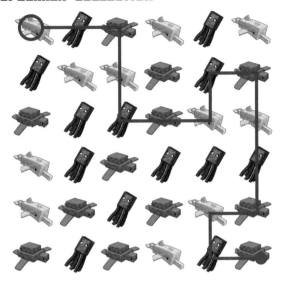

PAGE 20,
SPELLING BEE #2

_O_T	_E_G	_S_A	_I_Z	MINE	_U_L
_I_O	_A_W	Z_K	_E_D	_O_D	_A_F
_R_O	_Y_A	_U_R	_O_K	_I_H	_E_B
_I_X	_P_E	_A_Y	J_I	_E_K	_O_O
_A_Q	_O_Z	_F_U	_Y_V	_U_N	_A_T
_U_F	_I_T	_W_O	_A_V	_E_K	_U_P

PAGE 21,
CHEST QUEST

Crazy Q is the only player to find the chest.

PAGE 22,
FROG FITNESS

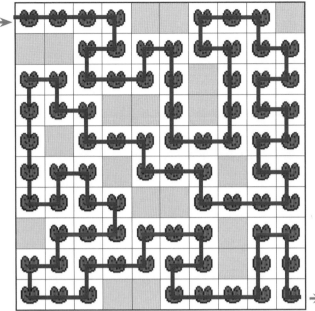

PAGE 23,
ENCHANTÉ

START

FINISH

PAGE 24,
HOP TO IT #2

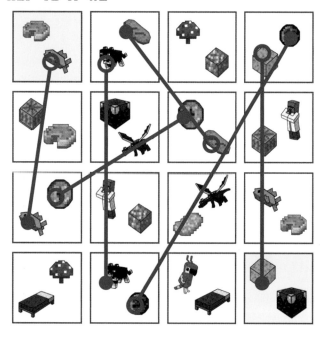

PAGE 25,
NAP TIME

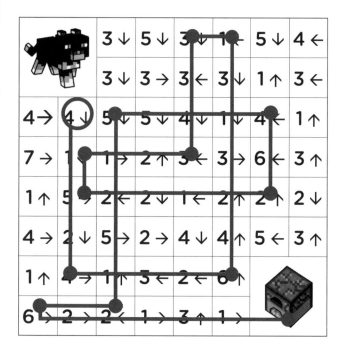

PAGE 26,
DIAMOND DASH

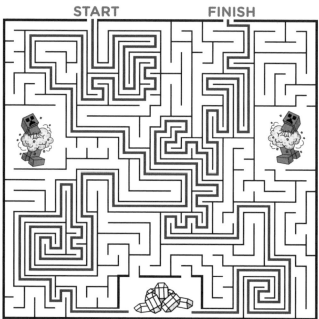

PAGE 27,
GOOD TRADES BAD TRADE

Lexi - Librarian
Chase - Blacksmith
Camille - Cleric
Ryan - Nitwit
Bailey - Butcher

PAGE 28,
SMOOTHIES FOR SIX

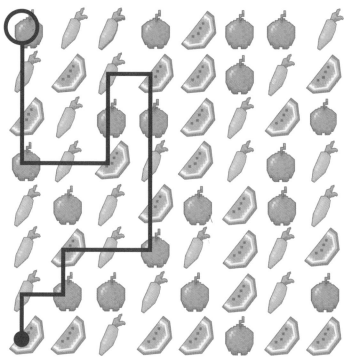

PAGE 29,
SPELLING BEE #2

PAGE 30,
INTO BATTLE

Scarrr - Shulker

Clash - Evoker

Jaction - Ghast

Attax - Drowned

PAGE 31,
CACTUS CROP COLLECTION

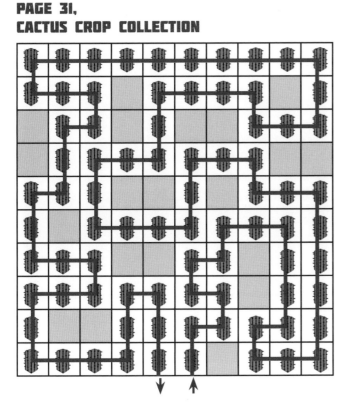

PAGE 32,
LAVA KNOWLEDGE

START

FINISH

PAGE 33,
HOP TO IT #4

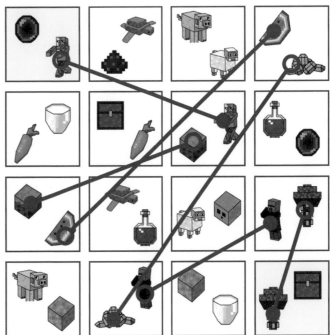

PAGE 34,
LOST BEACON

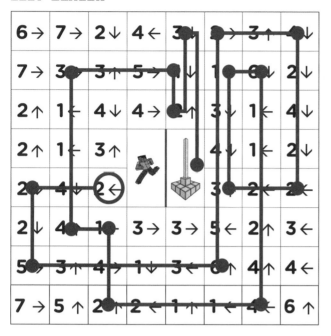

PAGE 35,
AN ENCHANTED HOE

START

FINISH

PAGE 36,
A VERY SMART PIG (AND A FUNNY GIRL)

EINSWINE

PAGE 37,
MAIN COURSE MIX-UP

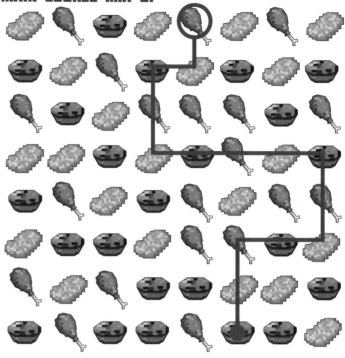

PAGE 38,
SPELLING BEE #4

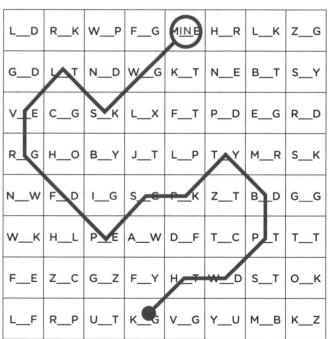

PAGE 39,
A SECRET MESSAGE

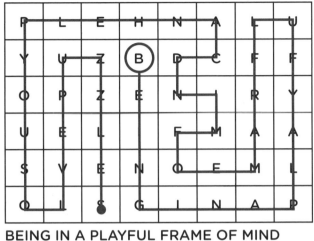

BEING IN A PLAYFUL FRAME OF MIND CAN HELP YOU SOLVE PUZZLES.

PAGE 40,
BEDS WANTED!

Poppy and Diego find beds.

PAGE 41,
COBWEB DREAMS

PAGE 42,
SADDLE UP!

PAGE 43,
HOP TO IT #5

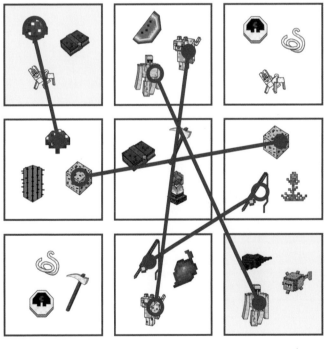

PAGE 44, THE PEARLY PATH

3↓	4→	2→	2↓	1←	4↓	3↓
3↓	5→	2↓	5↓	1↓	5←	3←
6→	3↓	3←	2→	3↓	2→	2↓
2→	3↑	3↓		3←	2↓	1↓
1→	4↑	3↑	1↓	1←	4↓	4↓
3↑	3→	5↑	2↑	4←	3←	2→
4↑	5↑	3→	1→	3↑	5↑	5←

PAGE 45, MOB HOUSE

START   FINISH

PAGE 46, SCAVENGER HUNT FINDS

Ariel - 3

Brandon - 4

Erika - 1

Todd - 2

Suzy - 5

PAGE 47, MOOSHROOM SHEARING

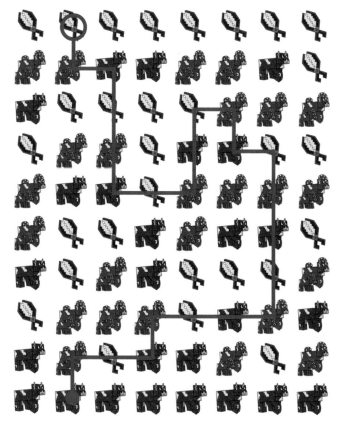

PAGE 48, SPELLING BEE #5

MINE	_AL_	_UD_	_IK_	_AB_	_OC_	_IY_	_OZ_
_O_	_OG_	_AF_	_AC_	_UH_		_OI_	_EH_
_IJ_	_IM_	_UK_	_AU_	_GV_	_UM_	_AO_	_YL_
_TL_	_SN_	_US_	_AK_	_OM_	_EO_	_IP_	_UT_
_AT_	_LL_	_UQ_	_EL_	_IS_	_OT_	_UU_	_IC_
_IV_	_IK_	_AN_	_OW_	_U_	_O_	_OP_	_AX_
_OZ_	_PR_	_UP_	_A_	_AY_	_RT_	_IB_	_AI_
_UW_	_OL_	_CH_	_EV_		_AE_	_ID_	_OB_

PAGE 49,
WHERE AM I?

Ambler and Drifter - Jungle

Gad2222 - Deep Ocean

Journey-Man - Arctic

PAGE 50,
'NOTHER NETHER STAR, PLEASE

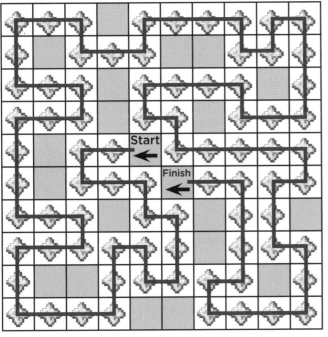

PAGE 51,
CHEST JESTS

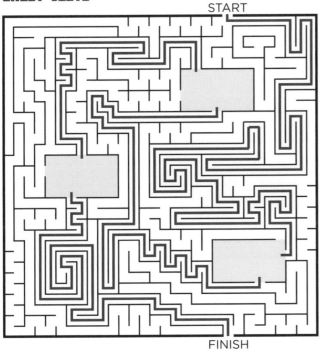

PAGE 52,
HOP TO IT #6

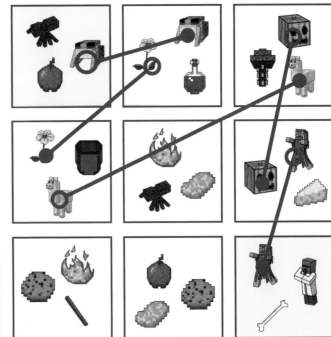

PAGE 53,
QUICK! YOU CAN SAVE US ALL!

3 →	8 ↓		6 ↓	2 ↓	1 ←	8 ↓	2 ↑	5 ↓
7 →	3 ↓		2 ←	2 ↓	5 ←	6 ↓	2 ↓	6 ←
2 ↑	4 ↓	2 ←	1 →	3 →	4 ←	1 ↓	5 ↓	2 ←
1 ←	7 →	3 →	4 ↓	1 ↓	6 ←	3 ←	3	7 ←
4 →	1 ←	2	3 ←		4 ↑	2 ←	3 ←	3 ←
5 ↑	2		1	2 ↓	1	5 ↑	3	7
2 →	4 →	1 ↑	5 →	2 ↑	4 ↑	4 ↓	2	4 ↑
1 ↑	4		1 ←	4		1 ↑	7 ←	6 ←
5 →	2 ↑	3 ↑	7 ↑	4 ↑	3 ↑	3 ←	5 ←	4 ↑

75

PAGE 54,
GO FOR GLOW

FINISH

START

PAGE 55,
LAUGH LINES

KARAT CAKE

PAGE 56,
MOB SCHOOL CARPOOL

PAGE 57,
SPELLING BEE #6

B_P_	S_B_	P_L_	R_P_	S_F_	F_D_	M_NE	Z_G_
J_B_	P_M_	K_B_	C_C_	W_G_	L_M_	T_G_	F_N_
D_D_	H_R_	R_R_	Y_D_	P_P_	G_M_	S_Q_	K_L_
W_B_	H_V_	P_T_	Z_P_	W_S_	A_P_	T_O_	Q_T_
C_T_	O_N_	K_T_	F_B_	U_P_	F_V_	E_J_	H_K_
A_B_	C_M_	D_G_	W_R_	R_H_	Z_M_	Y_D_	N_C_
G_X_	T_M_	F_Y_	H_Q_	B_T_	G_V_	G_D_	J_M_
N_R_	W_G_	L__	S_C_	C_H_	T_F_	G_H_	C_E_

PAGE 58,
CHICKEN HERDING

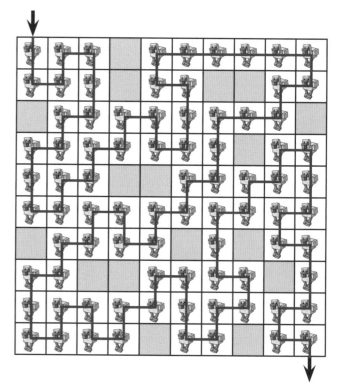

PAGE 59,
SHEDDING LIGHT ON REDSTONE TORCHES

START   FINISH

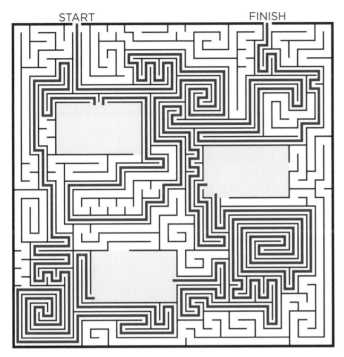

PAGE 60,
HOP TO IT #7

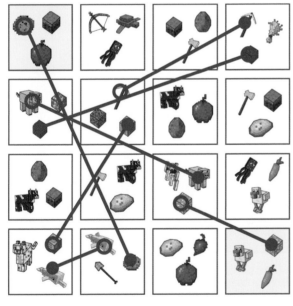

PAGE 61,
GO FOR THE GOLD

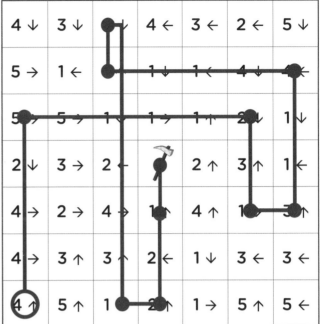

PAGE 62,
PURSUING PRISMARINE

START

PAGE 63,
UNDEAD HUMOR

BRAINS!

PAGE 64,
EGG HUNT

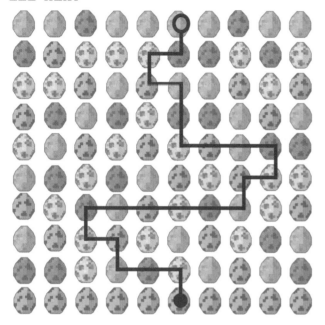

PAGE 65,
SPELLING BEE #7

C R AFT	__OWD	__IDE	__UMP	__ESP	__YPT	__EPE	__ALK
__IMP	__ONG	__ASH	__OSH	__ESS	__USE	__EAT	__OON
__UDE	__ITE	__UMB	__ALM	__UGE	__ANE	__OLE	__AIL
__UEL	__OUG	__IFT	__EST	__EWL	__USH	__ISP	__EAN
__UST	__ACE	__IME	__ANG	__ODA	__ATE	__UBE	__ACK
__EEP	__PLE	__YNG	__AWL	__EAM	__ILF	__OPT	__EEK
__OLY	__EDO	__IFY	__OAP	__IGE	__IFE	__AVE	__ANK
__ELT	__UFF	__SPY	__ILL	__AZE	__OWN	__GST	__LPY